Introduction

Multiculturalism is a hot issue these days. North American educa cultural, physical and racial differences between children and groups o must be more then a fad or trend. Multicultural education is more than a week-long teaching "unit." The goal is to explore the beauty of all people and every individual, and to encourage awareness, respect and acceptance of the self and others.

The North American cultural heritage is a treasure chest filled with priceless heirlooms. In many larger communities we can travel the world without leaving the boundaries of our city.

Unfortunately, in ignorance people cling to stereotypes and the resulting racial intolerance is an ugly and recurring phenomena. We have the opportunity to educate, explore and explain and in so doing we can not only remove ignorance, but invest in cultural heritage.

Cultural education must be sensitive and considerate. Please do not single out little Gino and ask him about pasta; do not ask eight year old Indira about marriage customs in India; and do not ask Abraham how Christmas is celebrated in Israel. Explore these subjects, but explore them as an entire class. Create an atmosphere where each child can feel special without being singled out by perhaps unwanted attention.

This is not to say that a student from a specific culture cannot contribute his or her own personal insights as part of the exploration. An individual perspective is often a highlight of the entire school year. Many children, normally shy and withdrawn, will begin their involvement in the classroom through just such kinds of discussions. After all, they are the experts. You as a teacher must create the kind of environment in which students feel comfortable contributing. Such an environment is open, non-critical and respectful. Allow your students to reveal their insights and receive the insights of others.

Start multiculturalism as early as possible. Start in preschool. As a beginning, put international cookbooks in the cooking centre, have a wide range of clothing in the dramatic centre, and label classroom objects in an assortment of languages. These are simple but effective ways to show children that different people make up the world. We have included a potpourri of other ideas at the end of this book.

Involve families in your classrooms. Involvement might range from a grandparent guest speaker focusing on ethnic festivals or folk tales to an invitation to submit favourite "snack" recipes for classroom trial or as part of a cookbook your students will "publish." Make parents aware that you value and respect the cultures of all your students through newsletters, international cookbooks, a family open house and ethnic crafts and stories. The possibilities for including families into your classroom are endless and exciting.

One danger in "teaching" multiculturalism is the tendency for teachers to ignore the dominant classroom racial group. Perhaps your class is made up of ninety percent English-speaking, white children. Resist the temptation to ignore that group and focus on all of the "unique" students because by doing so you will send a message to all of your students that the dominant culture is the "right" one, the "natural" one, and therefore does not need to be explored.

Finally, have fun! Tell stories from around the world, make crafts, explore cultural festivals, listen to music, cook international foods, read poetry, watch cartoons from other countries...explore, explore, explore!

I hope you enjoy the ideas in this guide. We have begun by focusing on the classroom as a community to establish a base from which to begin our explorations. We then reach out to the rest of the world through general, common and fun categories such as foods, games, clothes and crafts. Our plan is to explore the world and experience its riches in order to know ourselves and our community a little better.

I enjoy talking and working with teachers. If you have any comments or ideas please write me.

Toby Valensky

30 Northland Road
Waterloo, Ontario CANADA
N2V 1Y1

6300 Inducon Corporate Drive
Sanborn, NY
14132-0242

Published by Roylco Limited Waterloo, Ontario Canada
Roylco Inc. Sanborn NY 14132-0242

Printed In Canada

Contents

Chapter One
All About Me

Proceed from the familiar to the unfamiliar. This piece of common sense is invaluable for creating multicultural awareness in your classroom. Begin your exploration of the world by exploring your classroom. Your students will create bonds as they share experiences, and will establish respect for each member of their classroom community.

One benefit of these activities and crafts is the opportunity for the teacher to learn about each child, his or her family, preferences and dislikes. I remember talking to a young man about his first year of school. He came to Canada from India and started in the second grade. Not being familiar with East Indian names, the teacher accidently inverted the student's surname and given name. For an entire year that little boy was called by his last name. He was unaware of North American customs and at first thought that all students were referred to by their last names. Once he understood a mistake had been made he was too embarrassed to correct the teacher. What an unfortunate way to be introduced to a new school system and a new country.

We have organized this section by beginning with the individual, moving to the family, and ending with the neighbourhood. All of the participants in the class will have an opportunity to examine their personal uniqueness and to look at the uniqueness of others. As the teacher you may be introduced to many different cultures through your students.

Goals:

- Establish a beginning point from which to securely explore the world.
- Foster respect for differing cultures, abilities and lifestyles.

All About Me

Activity: All About Me Book.

Materials:

- paper
- crayons
- assorted craft supplies
- stamp pad (optional)
- book binding method: stapler, hole punch and yarn

Method: Make this a week long activity. Set aside an "All About Me" period in which children can draw a picture, paste photos from home, write descriptions that relate to the day's theme. **Hint:** Play music from different cultures during these periods. At the end of the week compile the pages, decorate a book cover and bind the books. **Hint:** Remember to include on the cover, "Written by..." and "Illustrated by..." Use this opportunity to discuss book publishing, book stores, and libraries. Visit the biographical section of the library.

Suggested daily themes: My Favourite Place; My Favourite Food; My Family; My Favourite Game; My Favourite Holiday...
Hint: Whenever possible label the pictures for younger students, Nana's House, Pizza...

Cover suggestions: 1. Children can design a self-portrait. Make mirrors available; look at self-portraits of famous artists: Picasso, Van Gogh, etc. 2. Use a stamp pad to make fingerprints for the cover. Children can draw a face on each fingerprint to represent their family members. Talk about the uniqueness of all fingerprints. 3. Children can trace their handprint. At the end of the year they can compare the size of their hand to the hand print on the cover. 4. Take a photograph of each child, have it developed. Children can glue their picture onto the cover of their book. **Hint:** Let each student title their own book.

Follow-up Activities: Children can share their books with classmates by "reading" them in small circle groups. Alphabetize the books and place them on a special shelf in your classroom library/reading centre.

Other All About Me Ideas

Make a handprint tree! Students trace and cut out their handprints from different coloured craft paper. Write each child's name on the handprint. Cut out or paint a tree trunk and arrange the hands as leaves. Use this tree throughout the year to discuss how trees change during fall, winter, spring and summer seasons.

Handprint Tree

Make show-and-tell treasure boxes! Each child decorates a shoe box by covering it with craft paper, painting, using stickers, gluing cut-outs, etc. Discuss how each person has their own treasures that are important and priceless to them. Ask the children to take their box home once each week, fill it with a personal "treasure" and bring it back to school. In small groups children can discuss their objects and explain why they are important.

Make an "All About Me" bulletin board! Provide children with name tags at the beginning of the year for them to decorate. Once you have memorized everyone's name, use the tags to decorate the board. Periodically ask children to bring in pictures from home or decorate the board with outstanding pieces of art, childhood pictures of parents, grandparents and siblings, classroom photographs, etc.

All About My Family

Children naturally believe that every family is just like the one they come from. It is very important to promote an understanding and an appreciation for all kinds of families. Children must learn that a family can be made up of people both related and unrelated to the child. Be sensitive to the different types of families children come from - large, small, nuclear, extended, single-parent, foster family, etc.

Activity: Family Portrait

Materials:
- reproducible body shapes and sizes
- hair-coloured yarn
- assorted craft papers, scissors
- people-coloured paper, crayons
- background paper, glue

Method: Reproduce body shapes (see chapter six) or draw your own on a variety of people-coloured paper. Children can select the colours and shapes they want and cut them out.

Each child can design clothes for the figures and cut them out of the craft papers. Detail can be added with crayons and markers. Arrange and glue the people to the paper background. Help the children label each member with the appropriate name. Watch for variations on similar names i.e., Oma, Mimi, Grandma, Babci, Nana, Grandmére. **Hint:** Frame these portraits. Make a border of buttons, stickers, shells, etc.

Encourage your students to "introduce" their families via the portraits in small discussion groups. **Hint:** Your students will love to dictate an autobiography to an older student especially invited into the class for the purpose.

Follow-up Activities: Sharing family portraits provides an excellent opportunity for exposing children to different languages. 1. Make up a chart which lists the same family member name in different languages. For instance, list all the words that are equivalent to the English "mother." **Hint:** One language may have more than one word for mother depending on the different cultures which share that language, i.e., mother, mum, mom, mamma.... Resist the temptation to start each column of your chart with the English word which perpetuates the myth that English is the "correct" language. 2. Make similar charts using the names of brothers, sisters, pets, last names, etc. In small groups, alphabetize each child's surnames and then look them up in the phone book.

Make a classroom art gallery. **Hint:** Be sure to place plaques under each work of art complete with artist's name, work's name, date, etc.

Visit local art galleries. Research portraits from other countries and historical periods. Compare pictures of children from long ago to pictures of children today. As a class, discuss the differences and similarities of these portraits.

Other Suggestions:
Make a family album. This would be similar to the "All About Me Book" featuring an illustration on each page of a different family member. Write the name of each person and interesting facts for each page. **Hint:** Children from smaller families may want to fill their pages with pictures of favourite activities the family enjoys together or separately.

Make a family bulletin board using actual photographs children bring in from home. Make a border using cut out handprints or the word "family" printed in as many languages as possible. **Variation:** Post the photographs on the handprints that make up the handprint tree and rename it "Family Tree."

Talk about family traditions such as the way we celebrate birthdays. Some children may eat special or favourite foods on their birthdays; others may celebrate by breaking open a piñata. Some of your students may refer to such celebrations as their "name day." Make a chart of different ways to celebrate. **Hint:** Include a list of the words equivalent to "Happy Birthday" in other languages.

All About My Neighbourhood

Encourage children's awareness that they are part of a larger community outside the school.

Activity: Neighbourhood Map.

Materials:
- large sheet of paper and felt-tipped pens.
- empty boxes, cereal, shoe, milk cartons, etc.
- craft paper
- scissors
- glue

Method: Take a walk around the neighbourhood with your students. Take note of different businesses, churches, homes, parks and other areas of interest. **Hint:** Bring along a camera and take photographs. Use these photos as points of reference. Later, use them as part of a community bulletin board border.

When you return, draw a map of the area with your students centring on the area around the school and add the places you saw on your walk. **Note:** Make the map simple or complex in relation to the developmental level of your class.

Hint: Use your map to introduce or discuss road safety, methods of transportation, north, south, east and west, left and right.

Variation: Make a three-dimensional map of the neighbourhood by covering milk cartons, cereal boxes, etc. with different colours of craft paper to represent buildings. Draw an unlabelled map on a large sheet of paper. As a class, label the streets and landmarks. The students can then place their box-buildings on the map in relation to the streets. This is a great way to introduce home addresses to early grades students. Ask your students to write their address on their box-building and place it in the correct area of the map.

Use this map exercise as a starting point to discuss how different children get to school in the morning; by car, bike, on foot, bus, etc. Make a graph of all the different ways children travel to school.

Follow-up Activities: Place your map in the building block centre of your classroom and encourage children to build new buildings, create the ideal playground, etc.

Other Suggestions: Adopt a tree in the neighbourhood and visit it throughout the year. Note the seasonal changes and discuss them in groups. Periodically clean up under the tree and discuss conservation and ecological issues. Talk about shade and light and the environment. Enjoy a spring picnic, stories, or games under the protection of its shade.

Go on a garbage walk and pick up litter in your neighbourhood, favourite park, playground, school yard, etc. At the end of the walk weigh the amount of garbage you have collected and discuss other ways to improve the environment. This activity is a great way to show the positive effects a group can have when they work together on common goals.

Start a community outreach program. Perhaps there is a retirement home in your community. Start with correspondence and lead to meetings. Invite seniors into your classroom to tell stories or enjoy a snack. Exchange visits before any special occasion such as Valentine's Day, Hallowe'en, Hanukkah, etc., with little handcrafted cards and gifts.

As an integrated art/language activity, children can draw their home and describe it in a poem. They can learn all the different names for home designs; split-level, bungalow, two-story, condo, co-op, apartment, town-house, etc. Children can architecturally design their own dream home and write a description focusing on why it is perfect for them.

Provide children with a variety of pictures of home design and make a graph by asking students to identify their home design and charting the results. **Hint:** Include designs from all over the world; houseboat, pagoda, farmhouse, tent, etc. **Note**: This type of exercise is especially effective if most children in your class live in very similar homes as it will expose them to unique and different cultures.

Chapter Two
Celebrations

In North America there are a great number of people who celebrate many different religious and cultural traditions. Explore some of these celebrations as part of your curriculum.

Explore imaginative mask making through Mardi Gras celebrations. Throw a birthday bash during Chinese New Year. Express gratitude for the harvest during the festival of Divali. What an exciting way to explore the richness of other cultures and religions with your students!

The celebrations in this section cover a period from September through April and can be introduced chronologically or can be tailored to meet the needs of your class. For example, Kwanzaa, an African harvest festival which occurs on December 26th, can be celebrated with your students in the fall or winter.

Goals:
- Show the universality of many celebrations.
- Allow children to experience and thereby understand other cultural holidays.

Fall Festivals

Festivals of thanksgiving for the harvest are celebrated in countries throughout the world.

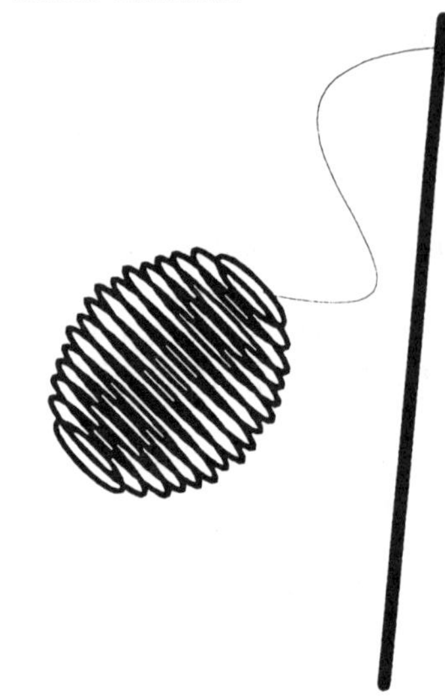

China - The Harvest Moon Festival

This Chinese festival is held on the day when the moon is full during September or October of each year. Usually held outdoors, this is a joyous celebration for a bountiful harvest. The festivities include dances, hymns of praise, poetry readings and a lantern parade.

Activity - Moon Lanterns

Materials:
- coloured yarn
- 12" (30 cm) thin stick or dowel
- white glue
- round balloon

Method: Blow up and tie one medium sized, round balloon for each child. Pre-cut twenty lengths of yarn for each student at least 20" (50 cm) long. The children drag or carefully dip the yarn into the glue then wrap it around the balloon. Let the glue dry overnight. The teacher can pop and remove the balloon. Hang the "moon" from the stick by attaching it with the string. Have a parade!

Follow Up Activity: Research and compose traditional and modern forms of Chinese poetry.

Vietnam - Trung-Thu

According to the Vietnamese calendar, Trung-Thu, a children's festival culminating in a lantern parade, is held on the 15th day of the 8th month. In North America it may be celebrated in August, September, or October.

Trung-Thu Lantern

Activity - Paper Lanterns

Materials:
- craft paper
- yarn, scissors,
- hole punch, stapler

Method: Fold a sheet of craft paper in half lengthwise. Mark lines on the paper about 1/2" (1.5 cm) apart beginning at the folded edge and continuing up to 1" (3 cm) from the top. Cut along these lines. **Hint:** As a timesaver, purchase pre-cut weaving mats.

When the papers are ready, unfold. Bring the short sides together, and staple at top and bottom. Punch a hole on each side and string with yarn to make handles. **Hint:** Put a "light" inside your lantern by covering a toilet paper roll with yellow craft paper to place inside the lantern, stapling the lantern together around the paper roll.

North America - Thanksgiving

A North American celebration of thankfulness, this holiday is celebrated on the second Monday in October in Canada and observed on the fourth Thursday in November in the United States.

Activity - Turkey Centrepiece

Turkey Centrepiece

Traditional North American Thanksgiving Day feasts include a turkey - here's one you can make and use to decorate your table.

Materials:
- round balloon
- craft paper
- glue, scissors

Method: Draw the turkey's head, tail and feet onto the craft paper. Cut out and decorate as you wish. Blow up the balloon. Attach the turkey's head to the knotted end, its tail to the back and large feet on the bottom.
Hint: Throw the turkey up in the air and watch as it lands on its feet.

Activity - Thanksgiving Book

Fasten together a number of pages to make a book. On each page have students draw items they are thankful for. **Hint:** Don't forget the special people in their lives.

India - Divali

Also known as Diwali, this important Hindu celebration from India occurs in October or November of each year. Divali is known as the Feast of Lights because of the many "dipas" - little clay oil lamps or candles that are placed everywhere. For many Hindus, Divali marks the beginning of a new year.

Activity - Dipas (Clay Candle Holders)

Materials:
- 1 cup (250 ml) cornstarch
- 2 cups (500 ml) baking soda,
- 1 1/2 cups (375 ml) water
- paint
- small round wax candles (optional)

Method: In a saucepan stir together cornstarch and baking soda. Add water, mixing until smooth. Cook over medium heat, stirring constantly until mixture resembles slightly dry mashed potatoes. Turn onto plate, cover with damp cloth and cool. When cool, knead until soft and pliable. Store unused clay in airtight bag or container in cool place for up to 2 weeks. Knead before using.

Give each child a small ball of clay to be fashioned into a bowl- like candle holder. Dry for 24 - 36 hours, turning occasionally. Paint or decorate as desired. Use the dipas during your Divali celebration after you have added small wax candles or tube-shaped candles that the students have made from paper. **Hint:** Use this as an opportunity to remind students of fire safety rules.

Activity - Divali Party

In North America many East Indian stores may be decorated with coloured electric lights during Divali. String coloured lights up in your room and have a party. Serve some traditional food such as Chapattis (see Foods section). **Hint**: Remember at Hindu festivals the preparation and serving of special food is often an important part of the celebration, so make this an exciting part of your party!

Other Harvest Activities

October 16th has been declared World Food Day by the United Nations. Talk about the importance of food in our lives as you recognize this day with your students. Discuss the lack of food many people face. Explore ways in which we can share what we have with others. Have a fundraising activity as a class and use the money to buy food for others - supporting a local food bank for example. Plan a field trip to a grocery store or market and choose appropriate foods together. **Hint:** Remember you may have some children in your class who are on the receiving end of these food baskets - be sensitive to them.

Set up a market in your dramatic play area. Provide tables or carts with harvest vegetables such as pumpkins, apples, corn and squash. **Hint:** Include harvest foods from around the world such as the yellow, red or white Chinese pumpkins or dark green Jamaican pumpkins. Include a scale to weigh the produce. Add play money or provide items such as clothes, toys, beads, etc. which students can use to barter for food.

Some of these food items can be used later as snacks or may be included in your harvest soup (see Food section).

Winter Festivals

These festivals are often a joyous time of celebration in communities around the world. One common theme running through many of these festivals is light - symbolizing the human spirit and the divine.

Jewish - Hanukkah

Hanukkah is an eight day Jewish holiday to celebrate religious freedom and the rededication of the temple after the defeat of Antiocus IV and his forces. During this festival, a candle is lit each day at sundown. Hanukkah is celebrated in December.

Activity - Menorah (nine-branch candlestick)

Menorah

Traditionally, each candle or shamash is placed in a candlestick holder known as a menorah. One candle is lit on the first night; a second is lit on the second night... until on the ninth night when all the candles are lit.

Materials:
- toilet paper tubes
- masking tape
- yellow and orange tissue paper
- cardboard
- paint

Method: Each child can arrange the rolls in four pairs and one single. Keep the single roll full size and cut the four pairs down to four different sizes. The centre candle will be the tallest followed by the next largest pair...down to the smallest pair on each end.

Tape the tubes to a long strip of cardboard, then paint the menorah. When the paint is dry, stuff pieces of tissue paper in each tube to represent the flames.

Follow-up Activity: Research traditional Jewish symbols and use them to decorate the menorah.

Activity - Hanukkah Paper Chain Decorations

Materials:
- strips of blue and white craft paper
- glue

Method: Fold a paper strip over and glue the ends together. Slip the next strip through the first and secure the ends. Repeat, alternating blue and white rings which are the traditional Hanukkah colours. **Hint:** Make this a co-operative learning activity and have the students work in pairs or small groups. Hang the chains in your classroom as part of your Hanukkah celebration.

Activity - Gelt

During Hanukkah, children receive small gifts, usually "gelt" or coins. Hide some gold foil-wrapped chocolate coins around the room and go treasure hunting!

Mexico, Spain - Posadas

Celebrated from December 16th - 24th in Spanish and Mexican communities, this feast commemorates the journey of Mary and Joseph to Bethlehem, the site of Jesus' birth. The feast ends each evening with a piñata filled with treats for the children.

Activity - Piñata
The piñata is a large hollow container, often shaped like an animal. It is filled with treats and hung high above everyone's head. Blindfolded children take turns hitting it with a long stick until it cracks open and everyone rushes for treats.

Materials:
- a round balloon
- newspaper
- paste made from equal parts of flour and water
- paint
- decorations (streamers, tissue paper, craft paper, etc.)
- glue
- string
- wrapped up treats such as candies, coins or small toys

Method: Divide the class into small groups. Blow up and tie one balloon for each group. The children can tear newspaper into 2" (5 cm) wide strips and dip each strip into the paste. They should wipe off excess paste and smooth over the balloon. Continue this process until the whole balloon has been covered twice. **Hint:** This can be a messy activity, so remember to cover your work area with newspaper before you begin.

After the first application of papiér-mâché has dried, repeat the process a few times. Open the piñata by cutting a 5" (12.5 cm) round hole across the top of the piñata. Remove the broken balloon. Pierce two holes on opposite sides of the opening. Make a handle to hang the piñata by threading string through these holes and tying.

Children can paint and decorate their piñatas. Before closing the hole on the top of the piñata, fill it with treats. Let the fun begin! Blindfolded children can take turns hitting their piñatas with sticks until the piñatas break.

Hint: Choose a theme for each group to decorate their piñata; animals, fish, magic creatures...

Activity - Posadas Dramatization

Posadas is a dramatization of the pilgrimage of Mary and Joseph to Bethlehem. Act it out in your class. Two children can assume the roles of Mary and Joseph. Other children can mime the roles of the inn-keepers and refuse entrance to the couple. The entire class can celebrate Mary and Joseph successfully finding refuge by breaking open a piñata.

African American - Kwanzaa

A traditional African harvest festival, "Kwanzaa" is Swahili for "first fruits." This seven day festival begins December 26th but because it is related to harvest activities it could be included in a fall unit.

Kwanzaa is also a re-affirmation of African customs and traditions in North America. It celebrates the ties that bind African customs to the cultural and social history of African Americans.

Seven principles guide the Kwanzaa celebration - unity (Umoja), self-determination (Kujichagulia), working together (Ujima), sharing (Ujamma), purpose (Nia), creativity (Kuumba), and faith (Imani).

Activity - Kinara

The kinara is a seven branch candlestick that represents Afro-Americans, both living and historical. The candles - one black in the centre, three red on the right side and three green on the left - stand for the seven Kwanzaa principles. One candle is lit each night during the festival; beginning with the black and alternating from a green to red.

Materials:
- green, black and red craft paper
- glue
- yellow and orange tissue paper
- paper for background

Method: Have the craft paper pre-cut into seven strips. **Hint:** Practise seriation - cut the pairs of red and green strips in graduated lengths. A single black strip will be the longest. Give one set of strips to each child. They can arrange the pairs in sequence.

Pre-draw the candle holder onto the paper so that children can arrange and glue the strips (see Chapter Six). **Hint:** To extend this project make a template or stencil of the candle holder so that children can trace and cut the pattern out of craft paper.

After the candles are on, glue on the tissue "flames."

Activity - Kwanzaa Values

Observe one principle each day with the students. This could be done through group discussions, posing ethical questions, or writing essays.

Activity - Kwanzaa Table

In many homes during the Kwanzaa celebrations, family mementos are placed on a table. Things such as photographs, medals, wedding rings and other items that are part of a family story can be included. Use this as an opportunity to learn more about your students and their families. Ask children to bring in a family photograph or memento that relates to their personal history. Children can tell each other their tales while in small groups.

Invite parents to bring special items and visit the class and relate their stories. As a personal touch, you as the teacher, can also participate and show and tell your favourite story.

Hint: This is a great time to talk about respecting other people's property. Keep the photographs that children bring from home in a photo album to protect them from harm.

China - Chinese New Year

The celebration of a New Beginning, this festival is over 5,000 years old and involves feasting, lantern parades and the giving of gifts. In fact, it was traditionally the custom in China for everyone to celebrate their birthday on Chinese New Year.

Activity - Lai-See (Good Luck Money)

On Chinese New Year, children receive red envelopes filled with good luck money from family members.

Materials:
- white and red craft paper
- scissors
- coins (from around the world if possible)
- coloured pencils
- glue or gummed stickers

Envelope

Method: Fold a square piece of red paper to form an envelope by folding each of the three corners in towards the centre of the paper. Fasten with a dab of glue or gummed sticker.

To make paper money, have the students put the coins under a thin piece of white paper and rub over them with a coloured pencil. Cut them out and put in envelopes.

Variation: Make your own paper money! As a class make a list of the elements used in paper money, i.e. the numeral, the written equivalent, a picture, the scroll work, serial number, etc. Have children design their own paper currencies. Use this money for dramatic play. Research the history of money. Take a field trip to a bank. This is a great time to introduce the units of money, equivalent amounts, etc.

Hint: Remind children that in China only paper money is used for the envelopes because coins are thought to be unlucky!

Activity - Dancing Dragons

Part of the finale of the Chinese New Year celebration is the giant dancing dragon. Here are two suggestions for adding a dragon to your celebration.

1) Paper Dragon

Materials:
- colourful craft paper
- glue
- scissors
- felt-tipped pens

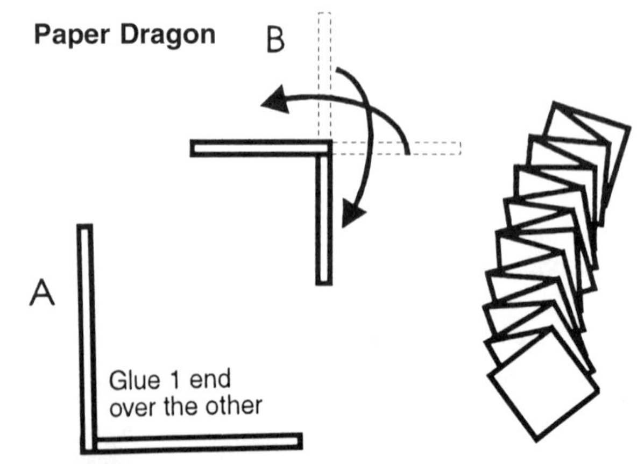

Method: Have the craft paper cut into long strips, at least 12" (30 cm) long and 1 1/2" (4 cm) wide. Place two strips together as illustrated. (A) Fold the first strip over, to the left - insert - glue them together where their ends overlap. (B) Fold the second strip up. (C) Continue in this way, folding one strip over the other. **Hint:** To make a longer dragon, when you near the end attach two more strips with glue. Use contrasting coloured strips.

When you have finished folding, glue the ends together. From a separate piece of craft paper, make a ferocious dragon's head from a separate piece of paper and glue to the end of the body. See Chapter Six for reproducible art.

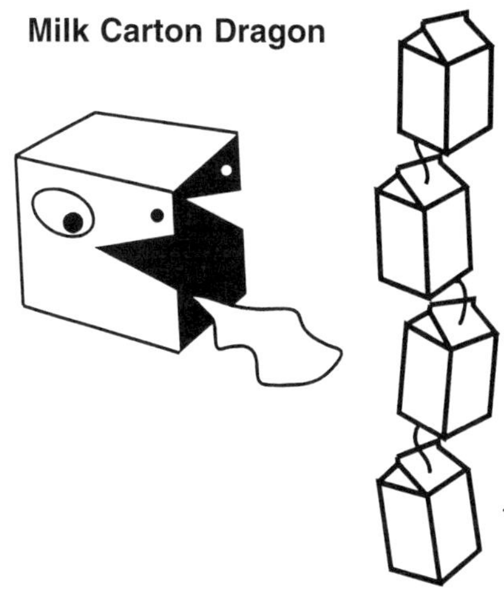

2) Milk Carton Dragon

Materials:
- milk cartons
- paint, decorative materials, gummed paper stickers
- tissue paper streamers, sequins
- string
- scissors
- white paper

Method: Cover each carton with white paper and then decorate as desired. **Hint:** Traditional Chinese dragons are very colourful. Use streamers, gummed paper stickers, sequins, etc. to cover as much of the box as possible. Decide on a colour scheme. For example, make the first box red; make the second box orange; then yellow, green, blue, purple.... When each child has made a carton, string them together end-to-end to form a long line.

To make the head, cut one carton in half to form a square box with one open side (do not use the end with the pop out spout). Starting from the open end of the box, cut two "V" slots on opposite sides to form an open jaw. Cover with paper and decorate. Be sure to include large eyes, nostrils and a tongue. Use string to attach the head to the body. **Hint:** Make eyes by decorating two cups from an egg carton and gluing them onto each side of the head; make a pointy red tongue from felt.

Play traditional Chinese music while the students hold onto their part of the dragon and dance around the room. As they dance, alternate holding the dragon above their heads, on their left side, right side, between their legs, etc.

Activity - Housecleaning

Part of the preparations for Chinese New Year include a thorough housecleaning to symbolize the "sweeping out of the old and welcoming in of the new." Involve the class in your New Year's preparations and clean the room together. Make it fun! Provide the children with brooms, brushes, dust cloths, spray bottles of water for the windows, and buckets. You'll be amazed at how much the children will enjoy cleaning up!

When you are finished cleaning share some traditional Chinese New Year fruits - an orange or tangerine. These are symbolic fruits. In Chinese, the pronunciation for "orange" and "wealth" are very similar. Likewise, the name for "tangerine" and "good fortune" sound alike.

France, The Caribbean, North America, Spain, Austria and more - Carnival

Originally a final feast before Lent, Carnival is celebrated in many different ways all over the world. The main events of Carnival usually take place the day before Lent begins which is called Shrove Tuesday or Mardis Gras (Fat Tuesday in French).

Research some of these celebrations. During Carnival in Rome and Venice, people form processions and toss flowers at their friends and neighbours to wish them luck in the future. In Spain, people march in processions wearing huge papiér mâché head-masks which parody historical characters and politicians. In Austria, you will find people marching in parades dressed as ghosts and witches.

Dancing and music are also important parts of Carnival. In Trinidad, they play calypso music to the beat of steel drums, in New Orleans they move to a jazzy beat and in Rio, they dance the samba.

Celebrate imaginative play with your students during your own masquerade festival!

Activity - Masks

Materials:
- craft paper
- aluminum foil
- glue
- paint
- paper plates
- paper bags
- scissors
- felt-tipped pens
- decorative materials: streamers, tissue paper, metallic paper, gummed stickers, feathers, etc.
- string, hole punch

Masks

Method: To make a paper plate mask, draw on the facial features and cut out the eyes. Decorate as desired. Hole punch at each side, add string. **Hint:** Use a theme such as animals or birds. Feather masks are very popular.

Method: To make a head mask, use the pattern illustrated to cut out a craft paper mask. Colour or paint and decorate the mask. Glue the three ends together and place over head.

Method: Other masks can be made using foil that has been pressed against the face to imprint nose, mouth, eye brows, etc. Remove the foil and cut out the eyes, mouth and nostrils of the mask. Add sequins, features, etc. Poke two holes on either side of the mask, add string.

Method: Make paper bag masks. Start with a large paper bag, cut out eye holes and decorate! Centre this activity around a theme such as famous people, literary figures, cartoon characters, etc.

Activity - Mardi Gras Party

Method: Provide scarves, blankets, ribbons, streamers, and jewellery for dress-up play. Children can act out their favourite circle time stories while wearing the mask of each character. Ask your students to name their mask-character. Write a biography of the character. Children can give little speeches while wearing the mask. Students can direct plays that they have written based on the mask-characters. Have a parade through the neighbourhood!

Activity - Carnival Band

Method: Make drums using empty coffee cans, other large tin cans or plastic tubs with lids. **Hint:** Cover sharp edges with tape. Decorate with foil, streamers and craft paper (see cover photograph). **Hint:** Pots and pans are also great drums for your celebrations.

Method: Make castanets for your dancers by taping the back of a flattened bottle cap to the thumb and another to the index finger and clicking them together.

Method: "Chac chacs" are used in Jamaica. These instruments are made from small, dried out gourds. Buy commercially prepared gourds that are already dried or dry your own for two weeks, make a hole, remove seeds, add some small stones and tape over the opening. Spray with varnish for durability.

Spring Festivals

These festivals occur all around the world and celebrate the renewal of life with the return of spring. Many of the foods and decorations used in these celebrations relate to a rebirth theme. Remember that in the southern hemisphere spring occurs during our fall. Add a geography theme to your celebration by having a spring festival during the fall months and examine your activities from an Australian or South American perspective.

Japan - Hina-Matsuri, Tango-no-sekku, Hana-Matsuri

In Japan, spring is a time of special children's festivals. Traditionally, Hina Matsuri - the Peach Festival - occurs on March 3 and is geared towards girls. On this occasion, doll collections are brought out and elaborately displayed. A tea party is held. The Boys Day of Japan, held on May 5, is called Tango-no-sekku and honours the sons of the family by flying one carp-shaped kite on a pole outside of the home for each son in the household. Today, these two celebrations are often combined into one large Children's Day both in Japan and North America.

As an activity children can design and make their own personal flags. Invite children to bring dolls or stuffed animals from home and enjoy a Japanese tea party. **Hint:** Be sure to have extra dolls on hand for children who forget theirs. Ask children to form small groups and introduce members to their dolls or animals. Ask for a biography of these characters. Decorate the "friends" with tissue paper flowers, streamers, etc.

The Japanese also celebrate spring with a flower festival called Hana Matsuri that occurs on April 8. This festival is celebrated in honour of Buddha's birthday.

Bring in a variety of flowers. Break the class up into small groups and give each group a flower. Ask the children to describe the flower: colour, number of petals, smell, size, etc. Make a chart comparing all of the groups' flowers. Children can make their own flowers with pipe cleaners or straws and pre-cut paper petals. Simply glue or tape one end of each petal onto the pipe cleaner or straw. Bring in a vase and display the flowers near the chart.

Activity - Koinobori

The carp has a special role in Japanese life. It represents strength and bravery; some are believed to be 100 years old when finally caught by fishermen. It is hoped that the sons will grow up to be strong and brave like the carp fish.

Materials:

- large paper bags
- stapler
- craft paper
- streamers
- scissors
- paint
- glue or tape
- string

Method: Close the bottom of a paper bag and fold each of the two corners in, stapling to secure. To make a mouth, cut a triangular hole in the front of the head. Paint and decorate the fish. **Hint:** Cut craft paper in circles to represent scales and glue in rows along the paper bag body. Attach streamers to the top end of the bag (the tail section).

Paint on eyes or make them from craft paper. Punch a hole above the mouth and thread a string through and knot it tightly. Hold the other end of the string and run and fly your kite. **Hint:** Afterwards, stuff the fish with newspaper and hang the kites up in your room as decoration.

Follow-up Activities: Research the carp. What is its life cycle? In what bodies of water are they found? What kinds of products do we get from carp? Children can write little descriptive stories about the imaginary life of their carp kite, either under the water or high up in the air.

Activity - Tissue Flowers

Materials:

- squares of tissue paper
- tape
- green craft paper
- straws
- stapler

Method: To create colourful flowers, stack two or three different coloured squares of tissue paper, then pinch the centre and twist. Wrap tape around the twisted end and insert into the straw or tape to the top of the straw. Cut leaves from green craft paper and staple to the straws. **Hint:** Use peach coloured paper and make "peach blossoms" to decorate your room during Hina Matsuri.

Iran, Afganistan, Iraq and some parts of the Middle East - Now Ruz

A celebration of creation and thanksgiving that occurs on March 21st in Iran, Iraq, Afghanistan and some parts of the Middle East. Preparations begin about two weeks before the equinox and include fire jumping, entertainment provided by a clown known as Haji Firuz, and the scattering of wheat, celery, and lentil seeds over water to soak and sprout. These seeds will later be used to symbolize the cultivation of the earth.

Activity - Sizdeh Bedar

The 13th day of Now Ruz is called Sizdeh Bedar. Traditionally, people want to be outside on this unlucky 13th day so they go on picnics. Visit a nearby park or playground or eat lunch outside at school as part of your Now Ruz celebration. Include some traditional Middle Eastern food such as pita bread. Read some of the tales from *One Thousand and One Arabian Nights* during your picnic. Back in class, draw pictures of the picnic or characters from the tales.

Activity - Haji Firuz

During Now Ruz, a clown called Haji Firuz makes people laugh during community gatherings. He sings, dances and wears make-up to hide his face. Using face paint and dress-up clothes, children can pretend to be clowns. **Hint:** Introduce clowns from other cultures. Look at French mimes and Russian acrobats.

Christian - Easter

A Christian festival, Easter celebrates Jesus coming back to life after his death on the cross. It occurs in the spring - also a time of new life and rebirth in nature.

Activity - Stained Glass Windows
In many older churches you will find stained glass windows depicting scenes from the life of Christ. The students will enjoy making a colourful stained glass window of their own.

Materials:
- craft paper
- glue
- waxed paper, same size as craft paper
- paint brushes
- tissue paper torn into small pieces
- scissors
- liquid starch in bowls

Method: Fold craft paper into eighths. On the longest side with folds (no raw edges), cut out a frame as shown in diagram. Open to reveal the window frame. **Hint:** For younger children you may wish to pre-cut the frames. Tape corners of waxed paper onto the table to prevent them from curling. Using paint brushes, apply a little liquid starch to the waxed paper. Place tissue paper pieces on it, and let dry. Glue the frame onto the waxed paper, trimming edges if neccessary. Hang finished artwork on the window to watch the sun shine through. **Hint:** Create a huge stained glass window by combining the finished windows of all of your students.

Activity - Easter Bonnets

Easter Bonnets

Easter Sunday commemorates the resurrection of Christ and is the most joyous day of the Easter celebration. Traditionally on this day, people would wear new clothes. Following this theme, make Easter Bonnets with the children.

Materials:
- paper plates
- craft paper
- yarn
- decorative materials such as tissue paper, brightly coloured craft paper, ribbons, gummed stickers
- glue
- hole punch
- stapler

Method: To make a paper plate hat, leave as is and decorate or make a wedge-shaped cut from the edge to the centre of a paper plate, overlap and glue or staple edges. **Hint:** For a steeper point make a wider wedge cut. Using a hole punch, make a hole at each side of the hat and string yarn through to be tied under the chin. **Hint:** Decorate hats with the tissue flowers made during Hana Matsuri.

Have an Easter Parade! Wearing your decorated bonnets, go on a walk through the school or neighbourhood!

Activity - Easter Eggs

For Christians, the egg is a symbol of Jesus' resurrection. Give each child an egg-shaped piece of craft paper, gummed stickers, felt-tipped pens and crayons and create Easter eggs. **Hint:** As a class, look at the elaborate eggs of the Ukraine or the Fabergé eggs of Russia.

Chapter 3
Cooking Activities

Food is more than a necessity of life; it is a focal point of culture and often forms a basis of religious celebrations and other social activities. Offering your students a variety of experiences with food is a terrific way to explore the tastes and customs of many cultures.

Goals:
- Explore the tastes and customs of other cultures through foods.
- Share knowledge about cultural eating habits.
- Recognize similarities and differences in foods across cultures.

Make activities with food part of the daily classroom experience. Here are a few ideas:

1. Dining styles vary around the world. Experiment with eating at tables, on floor mats or cushions, at low tables, or on trays.

2. Provide a variety of utensils and cooking equipment in your dramatic play area. Include such items as chopsticks, tongs, a mortar and pestle, a wok, ceramic spoons, etc. **Hint:** Perhaps parents have some interesting items at home such as pasta makers or tortilla presses and could give students a demonstration.

3. Ask the children to bring in empty food packages from home and start your own multicultural grocery store. Good items to include are empty spice containers or packages that have different languages on them.

4. Collect pictures of mealtime traditions and food from other lands and post them in your classroom.

5. Have a Classroom Community Feast with your students. Send home an invitation with each child inviting his or her family to a pot-luck dinner in the classroom. Ask each family to bring in a dish that is traditional to their family. **Hint:** Ask for a copy of the recipe as well so that you can compile a cookbook as a memento of this fun event.

Following is a comprehensive list of all cooking tools you will need to make the recipes in this section:

- baking sheet
- cutting board
- frying pans - electric and stovetop
- knife for cutting, slicing, and peeling
- mixing bowls
- sifter
- slotted spoon
- pastry brush
- wooden spoon
- can opener
- 8" (20 cm) square pan
- grater
- measuring cups and spoons
- saucepans - small, medium, large
- skillet
- spatula
- rolling pin

Bon appetit!

World Wide - Harvest Soup

Get everyone involved and make this potluck soup as a part of your harvest celebrations. Ask each child to bring an item from home such as carrots, celery, tomatoes, rice, noodles, bay leaves, etc. Together you can wash and chop up the vegetables and throw them all into the soup pot. Add water and salt, pepper, bouillon and let simmer until everything is tender. **Hint:** Start with a dry soup mix. Write down your "recipe." As a class decide on a name for your soup. Describe the taste, texture, colour, etc.

China, Japan, Vietnam, and many more Eastern countries - Rice

In China, rice is the foundation for many meals and is often eaten three times a day. Nutritious, inexpensive, and easy to prepare, rice can be eaten alone or in combination with other foods. **Some suggestions:** Sauté cooked rice in a frying pan with cooked meat, mushrooms, vegetables and soy sauce, or top cooked rice with butter, cinnamon and brown sugar.

Ingredients:
- 2 cups long-grained rice 500 ml
- 3 cups water 750 ml

Method: Put rice and water into a large saucepan. Do not cover. Bring to a boil on stove using high heat. Once rice is boiling, turn the heat down to medium and cook for 10 minutes. Lower the heat and cover the pan. Simmer for 20 minutes or until all the water has been absorbed. Fluff with a fork and serve.

Mexico - Tortillas

Ingredients:		
	- 2.5 cups corn flour	625 ml
	- 1 cup water	250 ml
	- 2 tsp. oil	10 ml
	- 2 tsp. butter	10 ml

Method: Mix corn flour with enough water to make a stiff dough. Give each child a small ball of dough, to be flattened with a rolling pin. **Hint:** Perhaps a parent has and can demonstrate a tortilla press to the students. Fry in a lightly oiled pan, turning until cooked. Brush with butter. Serves approximately 20 children. **Hint:** To make a nutritious, great-tasting tortilla snack, spread the tortilla with peanut butter and sprinkle with sunflower seeds or mixed diced fruit bits. Roll up and enjoy!

India - Chapattis

A form of unleavened bread, chapattis are often enjoyed on festival days or at wedding feasts in parts of India.

Ingredients:		
	- 2 cups whole meal flour	500 ml
	- 3 tsp. vegetable oil	15 ml
	- 1/2 cup water	125 ml
	- pinch of salt	
	- butter	

Method: Mix the flour, oil and salt in a mixing bowl. Gradually add water to prepare a thick dough. Knead the dough well and divide into six equal portions. Flatten each portion with a rolling pin. Roll out a circle approximately 1/10" (2mm) thick and 5" (12cm) across. Heat a frying pan on low. Cook the chapatti evenly, turning over to avoid burning. As it cooks it will puff up. Place the hot chapattis on a plate and spread with butter before serving. Makes six chapattis.

Caribbean - Rotis

Ingredients:		
	- 2 cups flour	250 g
	- 3 tsp baking powder	15 ml
	- 1/4 tsp. salt	1 ml
	- 1 cup water	250 ml
	- 2 tbsp. vegetable oil	25 ml

Method: Sift dry ingredients together. Add water in small amounts, mixing to form a stiff dough. Knead the dough thoroughly on a flat surface that has been sprinkled with flour. Shape into 5-6 balls. Cover with a cloth and let rise for 1 1/2 hours. Roll out the balls onto a floured surface. Heat frying pan to medium and lightly oil. Place rotis in the pan one at a time. Brush with oil and turn. Cook until brown. Serve warm. **Some suggestions:** Dot with butter and sprinkle with icing sugar or spread with peanut butter and add another Carribean treat - sliced bananas.

Christian - Hot Cross Buns

These delicious buns are a part of the Christian celebration of Easter.

Ingredients:		
	- 1 cup warm water	50 ml
	- 1 pkg prepared yeast	1
	- 2 tbsp. melted butter	30 ml
	- 2 tbsp. sugar	30 ml
	- 2 tbsp. mixed dried fruit	30 ml
	- pinch of salt	
	- 2 cups flour	500 ml
	- sprinkle of cinnamon and sugar, butter	

Method: Stir yeast into warm water until it dissolves. Set aside. In large bowl, mix remaining ingredients. Pour in yeast mixture and stir to form a firm dough. Place bowl in warm place for about an hour to let the dough rise. Cut dough and pat into eight buns. Sprinkle each bun with sugar and cinnamon and dots of butter. Cut a cross in each bun and place on a greased baking sheet. Cover with a cloth and let rise for one hour. Bake at 400F (200C) for about 16 minutes. Serve plain, buttered, or with a slice of cheese in the middle.

Native American - Navajo Fry Bread

Ingredients:	- 4 1/2 cup flour	1125 ml
	- 1/2 tsp. salt	2 ml
	- 2 tsp. baking powder	10 ml
	- 1 1/2 cup water	375 ml
	- 1/2 cup milk	125 ml

Method: Sift first three ingredients into a bowl. Stir in water and milk. Knead dough with hands. Pat or roll into circles approximately 5" (12cm) in diameter. With fingers, make a small hole in centre. Fry in several inches of hot oil in 400F (200C) electric frying pan. Dough will puff up and bubble. Turn when golden brown. Drain on absorbent paper and serve hot with honey.
Hint: To make tacos, spread with refried beans and top with shredded cheese and broil until cheese melts. Sprinkle generously with shredded lettuce.

Jewish - Latkes

A traditional food often eaten during Hanukkah, latkes are potato pancakes. They are generally served with sour cream, yogurt, or applesauce.

Ingredients:	- 3 large peeled potatoes	3
	- 2 tbsp. flour	25 ml
	- 1 small onion	1
	- 1 tsp. salt	4 ml
	- 2 beaten eggs	2
	- 1/2 cup oil	125 ml

Method: Coarsely grate the potatoes. Finely grate the onion and add to potatoes. Add beaten eggs, flour, salt. Stir, let sit 10 minutes to thicken. Press with a slotted spoon and pour off the excess liquid. Heat the oil to medium in the frying pan.

Drop the mixture by tablespoons into the oil. Fry the pancakes until lightly brown and crispy at the edges, then turn. Remove and blot on paper towels. Serve warm. Makes 16 - 18 latkes.

Rosh Hashanah Treats

One tradition of this Jewish New Year celebration is to eat an apple or other fruit dipped in honey, symbolizing everyone's wish for a year filled with sweetness.

Africa - Sweet Potato Candy

Make this traditional African treat as a part of your Kwanzaa celebrations.

Ingredients:	- 2 cups sweet potatoes	500 ml
	- 1 cup white sugar	250 ml
	- 1 cup brown sugar	250 ml
	- 1 tsp. lemon juice	5 ml
	- 1 cup marshmallows	250 ml
	- pineapple juice, orange juice or vanilla	

Method: Wash and boil the sweet potatoes. **Hint:** As a timesaver, use canned. Mash potatoes. Place in a pan and add lemon juice, sugar and marshmallows. Cook on low, stirring constantly until very thick. Set aside to cool. Add pineapple juice, orange juice or vanilla for flavour. Spoon into cups and serve.

North America/China - Fortune Cookies

In North America people often end a Chinese meal with fortune cookies. However, in China pastries and sweet dishes are reserved for special occasions and are rarely served with the daily meal. We have included a fortune cookie recipe because they are part of the Chinese-North American cultural experience, are fun to make and eat, and provide an opportunity for a writing activity.

Ingredients: - 4 egg whites 4
- 1 cup sugar 250 ml
- 1/2 cup melted butter 125 ml
- 1/2 cup flour 125 ml
- 1/4 tsp. salt 1 ml
- 1/2 tsp. vanilla 2 ml
- 2 tbsp. water 25 ml

Method: Prepare "fortune" messages on small strips of paper and fold them. **Hint:** Use a dictionary of quotations. Mix sugar and egg whites until fluffy. Add flour, salt, vanilla, water and butter to sugar mixture and beat well. Pour batter onto well greased cookie sheet in 3 inch (9cm) circles.

Bake for 8 minutes at 375F (190C). Bake until lightly browned, then remove one at a time. Place fortune in the middle of the cookie and fold. **Hint:** Fold while still warm to avoid cracking.

China - Almond Fruit Float

In China, a meal is usually ended with fresh fruit. For this recipe use any kind of fruit, fresh or canned. Mandarin oranges, sliced peaches, fruit cocktail and pineapple are a few delicious possibilities.

Ingredients: - 1 envelope unflavored gelatin 1
- 1 cup water 250 ml
- 1/2 cup sugar 125 ml
- 1/2 cup milk 125 ml
- 1 tbsp. almond extract 15 ml
- 14 oz. canned fruit with syrup 398 ml

In a saucepan, dissolve gelatin in water. Bring to a boil over high heat. Reduce heat to low. Add sugar and stir until dissolved. Stir in milk and almond extract. Mix well. Pour into a deep, square pan and allow to set at room temperature. Then cool in refrigerator. When cool, cut into cubes and serve topped with fruit and syrup. **Hint:** If there is not enough syrup with the fruit, make a syrup by mixing 1 cup of water (250 ml) with 3 tbsp. (50 ml) sugar and 1/4 tsp. (1 ml) almond extract. Chill and serve with fruit and gelatin.

Iran - Loz-e-nargil

A sweet treat, these are traditionally cut into diamond shapes.

Ingredients: - 1 cup sugar 250 ml
- 3/4 cup water 180 ml
- 3 cups unsweetened dessicated coconut 750 ml
- 1/4 cup chopped pistachio nuts 50 ml
- 2 tsp. shortening or margarine 10 ml

Method: Boil the sugar and water until the sugar is dissolved. Remove from heat and stir in coconut. Quickly pour mixture into a greased 8" (20 cm) square pan. Sprinkle nuts over top while mixture is still warm. Press lightly. Cool, cut and serve.

North America - Apple Snacks

In North America, apples are found in abundance during harvest-time. This recipe for Apple Snacks and the next recipe for Baked Apple Rings are two delicious ways to enjoy apples with your class.

Ingredients: - 2 qts apples 2 l
- butter or margarine

Method: Peel, core, and halve the apples. Shred apples coarsely and put on a greased baking sheet. Bake a 225F (110C), until dry. Remove from baking sheet with spatula; break into pieces and serve.

Baked Apple Rings

Ingredients:
- baking apples
- brown sugar
- cinnamon

Method: Peel and core the apples. Slice into thick rings and set on baking sheets. Each child may sprinkle 1 tsp. (4 ml) brown sugar and a little cinnamon onto an apple ring. Bake at 350F (180C) until sugar melts and rings soften. Cool and serve.

Italy - Muffulettas

Make these sandwiches together and then take them along on a picnic! **Hint:** Eat them for Sizdar - Bedah!

Ingredients:
- 1 loaf of round Italian bread
- 4 lettuce leaves
- 1 tbsp (15 ml) salad oil
- sliced green olives
- dash of vinegar
- 6 slices tomato
- 8 slices salami or pastrami
- 8 slices of cheese, such as mozzarella or provolone

Method: Slice the bread in half lengthwise. Wash lettuce leaves, pat dry and place on bread. Sprinkle lettuce with oil and vinegar. Lay the other ingredients on top in any order. Cover with top of bread and press down. Cut into 10 slices and serve.

Other Suggestions:

Bread is one food item that is made in many different forms while often containing the same basic ingredients. Make or buy different types of bread monthly as a snack item. Some suggestions are bagels, pitas, roti, chapatti, bannock and croissants. **Hint:** Let students add their favourite toppings such as peanut butter, jam or honey.

Make your own cook book! Have the children bring in their favourite recipes from home, add the ones you have made together in class and compile them. Children can design the book covers. Make copies for the children. Older children may write the recipes down for themselves. **Hint:** These make a good end of the school year memento for students.

Chapter 4
Games

Integrate the games and contests of different cultures into your classroom. Games require cooperation, participation and acceptance. They can be used as physically, emotionally and mentally challenging activities. Most important of all, they are fun!

In many cultures games are played at specific times during the year, seasonally or as part of a religious festival. Use these activities to introduce a cultural festival or play them throughout the year. Don't forget to include the universal children's games of hopscotch, jump-rope, kick-the-can, tag, and hide-and-seek in your curriculum.

Goals:
- Explore the fun and excitement of cultural games
- Foster cooperative skills and the acceptance of others

Indonesia, Malaysia - Stilts

Stilts are a great prop to have for use in a variety of activities and games. Use them in relays, obstacle courses, parades.

Materials:
- coconut
- hacksaw
- hammer and nail or drill
- knife
- string
- paint

Method: Using a hacksaw, cut the coconut in half. Drain and then scoop out the pulp with a knife and heavy spoon. If desired, decorate the shells with paint (see cover photograph).

Use the hammer and nail or the drill to make two holes three inches apart. Put a long length of string through the holes, knot and pull it to make a loop for use as a handle. Repeat with the other shell.

Children place one foot on each shell and "walk" by pulling on the string as they take each step.

Follow-up Activity: Save the pulp from the shells and use to make coconut chips! Slice the pulp into thin strips using a vegetable peeler and toast in a 350F (180C) oven for five minutes. Add salt or sugar and serve.

Iroquois - Peach Stone Game

This game is played during the Iroquois Mid Winter Festival. Traditionally the nature of this orderly game signified that all things were working as the Creator meant them to.

Peach Stone Game

Materials:
- peach stones or almonds (four - six)
- large salad bowl
- toothpicks or other markers
- paint or felt-tipped pens

Method: Using paint or a felt-tipped pen, colour one side of each peach stone. Put the stones in a bowl and toss them up into the air, catching them again in the bowl.

The player who has tossed the stones receives one point for each stone that lands with the marked side up. For each point, the player takes a toothpick. Each player may have ten turns and the player with the most toothpicks wins.

Follow-up Activity: Divide the class into groups with each having its own bowl and painted peach stones. After each participant has had a turn make a chart or graph of the results. Compare the graphs from all of the groups. Are there differences in the results of each group? As a class examine what reasons may have caused the differences.

Jewish - Dreidel

During the Hanukkah celebrations, children may play a game using the coins or "gelt" they have been given as gifts. This game is played using a dreidel box - a four sided spinning top with a Hebrew letter on each side. The letters are the first letters of the words "a great miracle happened here." This refers to the first Hanukkah when a small amount of oil burned in a holy lamp for eight days.

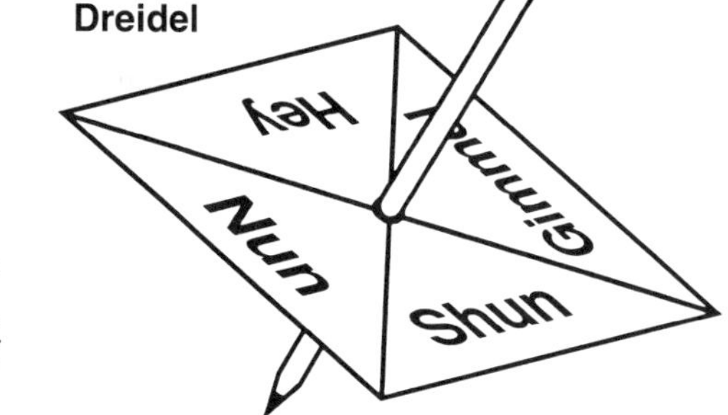

Materials: - 2" (5 cm) square piece of cardboard
- pencil
- felt-tipped pen
- "gelt" or other tokens

Preparations: Divide the square into four sections by marking it diagonally from corner to corner. In each section put one of the words Nun (none), Gimmel (all), Hey (half) and Shun (add to). Using scissors, poke a small hole in the centre of the cardboard and insert the pencil.

Method: Have each player place two tokens in the pot to begin the game. Then, each player in turn spins the dreidel and does whatever is indicated by the letter it lands on. For example, if a player lands on Nun, he or she takes nothing from the pot and the next player spins. If the dreidel lands on Gimmel, that player takes all of the tokens and each player puts two back into the pot. If Hey comes up, that player receives half the pot. When a player hits Shun, he or she must add one token to the pot.

The game ends when one person has all the "gelt" or after a pre-determined number of spins.

Follow-up Activities: As a class, research "the great miracle." It is an interesting story! Money or tokens are used for the "pot." This is a great time to introduce the different values of coins - nickel, dime, quarter, etc.

China, Cambodia, Indonesia - Dragon Game

This is a fun and exciting game that requires little preparation. A perfect activity to include in your Chinese New Year celebrations!

Materials: Musical accompaniment, use music from China

Method: As the music plays the children walk throughout the classroom or playground in single file, each holding onto the waist of the child in front. The first child in line is the dragon's head and the last child is its tail.

When the music ends, the head must try to tag the tail without breaking the line. As the tail avoids being caught, the rest of the participants try to help the head while keeping the "body" together.

Once the head has caught the tail, the head moves to the back of the line and the next person becomes the new head. **Hint:** Children can walk to different rhythms, hop, walk backwards, or side-step. As a group, decide which variation is the favourite.

Britain - Pancake Race

One of the most unusual Mardi Gras celebrations is the Shrove Tuesday Pancake Race in England. Traditionally, pancakes were made to use the dairy products forbidden during Lent. The first pancake race was in 1445 when a woman was so late for church that she forgot to put down her frying pan and ran all the way to church with her pancake! (Or so the story goes.)

Materials: - two or more small, lightweight frying pans
- scissors
- cardboard
- paint or gummed craft paper

Preparations: From cardboard, cut a circle that is a little smaller than the pan. Using paint or gummed craft paper, make each side of the "pancake" a different colour so that the judges are able to see it flip over.

Method: Give each racer a frying pan and pancake. Line the racers up behind the starting line. Place judges along the race path and have someone act as the bell ringer to signal the beginning of the race. As racers run along the path they must hold the pans out in front of them and flip their pancakes three times. The first person to cross the finish line after flipping the pancake three times, wins.

Follow-up Activities: Make a pancake relay race! Use a circular track so that racers finish at the starting line. Make up teams of three racers. Each racer must flip the pancake three times before completing the circle and passing the pan to the next racer.

After your pancake race, enjoy some real pancakes. **Hint:** Ask students to bring in their favourite pancake recipe from home. Together, make a list or chart of favourite pancake toppings.

Thailand - Takraw

A great game to encourage co-operation.

Materials: 1 soft ball or balloon

Method: Have the children join hands and stand in a circle. One person may toss the ball into the air. The participants must try to keep the ball in the air using their head, chest, knees, feet, or other body parts. **Hint:** To modify this game for young children, you may wish to have them use only their hands to keep the ball in the air. Play ends when the ball touches the ground.

Follow-up Activity: Make your own variations of this game. For example, isolate one body part at a time with which the children may bat the balloon. Using the left arm, right shoulder, or nose are just a few possibilities. For another variation, divide the children up into small groups and have them sit on the floor, leaning back on their hands for support. Provide groups with balloons that they are to to keep up in the air by extending their legs and kicking.

China - Lame Chicken

Materials: - sticks (10 per team)

Method: Divide the children into two or more teams. For each team, place ten sticks on the ground about a foot apart and in a parallel direction, resembling the rungs of a ladder. Each team stands in a line a few feet behind its row of sticks and, when the signal is given, the first person in every line must hop on one foot over each stick to the end of the row, pick up the last stick, hop back to the beginning and lay the stick down. Repeat this procedure with the other players. The first team to finish the sequence wins.

Nigeria - Jump over the Bag

Materials:
- rope
- old pillow case
- newspapers
- glue and fabric scraps

Method: Make a soft padded object by crumpling up old newspapers and stuffing them into an old pillow case. Tie the object to a rope that is at least 2 yds (2 m) in length. Decorate the bag with fabric scraps. **Hint:** Make a funny face and give it a name. Form a circle with the children and have one child stand in the centre holding the rope and attached object. Swing the rope slowly about a foot off of the ground. Everyone must jump over it to keep from being hit by the object at the end. Drop out if you are hit. The last person remaining takes the centre position.

Chapter Five
Clothing

Fill your dramatic centre with clothes and accessories from a variety of cultural groups. Choose garments that are representative of clothes worn everyday by people from many cultures rather than including only traditional holiday wear. Make these international fashions as a class project before adding them to your dramatic centre. The children will feel a sense of pride and mutual ownership as they wear their creations. The clothing and accessories included in this section are practical, easy to make, and fun to wear!

Goals: - Encourage acceptance of others and provide opportunities for individual expression while exploring clothing across cultures.

Cloth Selection

Provide a variety of fabrics from other countries for your exploration of clothes. Your local fabric store or used clothing stores are good sources. Look for colourful cloth, woven fabric, embroidery, lightweight cottons, fabrics that have been tie-dyed or batiked, etc. We have included instructions for creating some of your own colourful fabrics. If you choose to dye cloth as a fun class project, please ensure that there is adequate adult supervision - use this as an oppourtunity to invite some parents in as "helpers."

Follow-up Activities: Fabrics are an often over-looked but interesting aspect of culture. As a class, look at how fabrics are made; weaving, knitting, dying, sewing, etc. Look at different patterns, styles and fashions. Study how different people in the world have adapted clothes to meet their needs, from the Inuit in the north to the Bedouins in the desert.

Tie Dying

India, West Africa, Japan, and other parts of the world - Tie Dying

Materials:
- white cotton fabric
- cold water dye
- rubber bands or string and scissors
- rubber gloves
- soap and water
- two or more large pails
- clothes line for drying finished products
- paint shirts or other protective covering

Method: Prepare dye in a large pail, following the manufacturer's instructions. Provide each child with a piece of cotton cloth, about the size of a pillowcase. The children may bunch up sections of the cloth, wrapping a rubber band or tying a piece of string tightly around each section. **Hint:** For younger children you may wish to complete one large project together rather than using individual sections of cloth - use a bed sheet and have each child bunch up a section while an adult comes around to do the fastening. Wearing rubber gloves and protective clothing, soak the fabric in the dye. Rinse and wash the fabric in a pail of soapy water. Remove rubber bands or string and admire the design on the fabric. Hang cotton to dry, then iron.

Indonesia - Batik (wax writing)

Batik

Materials:
- white cotton cloth or handkerchief
- empty tin can
- old paintbrush
- rubber gloves
- paint shirts or other protective covering
- iron and newspapers
- saucepan
- parrafin wax or a bar of beeswax
- masking tape
- large pail
- cold water dye

Method: Prepare the dye according to the manufacturer's instructions. Place wax in the tin can and put the can in a saucepan of water. Melt wax by heating saucepan on low heat. Tape each child's piece of cloth onto a flat surface. Remove the can of melted wax from the saucepan and place on the table. Paint a design onto the fabric using the melted wax. Work quickly before the wax has cooled. Wearing rubber gloves and protective clothing, dye the fabric. Hang the fabric up to dry. To remove the wax, iron the fabric between sheets of newspaper - the wax will melt onto the paper. (Again, you may wish to modify this activity for younger children by working together on one larger project or perhaps inviting someone in to provide a demonstration of the art of batik.)

Other Suggestions:

Make your own colourful fabric by sponge painting a square of plain cotton with a combination of tempra paint and detergent. Or, design a pattern on fabric by potato printing. Simply wash a potato, cut in half, and carve a shape or symbol into the centre. Then, just dip and print!

Poncho

Mexico - Poncho

Ponchos are familiar in Mexico and South America but can be found throughout the world.

Material:
- 1 m (1 yd) square material
- scissors
- waterproof fabric markers or bits of fabric and glue

Method: Fold fabric in half and cut a "V" shape slit big enough for a head to slip through in the centre of the fold. Cut fringes along the bottom or ask students to make yarn tassels and attach them to the poncho. Decorate using waterproof markers or by gluing bits of fabric to form patterns or pictures.

India - Sari

Sari

Often made of silk or cotton, a sari is the traditional women's costume of India.

Materials: - 1 1/2 yds (1.5 m) of 3 ft (90 cm) wide fabric

Method: Take one end of the fabric and place it on the right hip, tucking the end into the waistband of your pants or skirt. Wrap it once around the body. The bottom of the fabric should just touch the floor. When you return to the front, make four or more accordian-like pleats in the fabric and tuck them into waistband. Take the remaining cloth in your left hand, passing it around your back to your right hand. Bring it back over the body at a slant, draping it over the left shoulder, allowing the rest of the cloth to rest gently down your back.

Sarong

South East Asia - Sarong

Sarongs are lengths of cotton often worn by people in South East Asia.

Materials: - 2 m (2 yd) length of fabric with edges sewn or safety pinned together

Method: Step into the centre of the ring of cloth, and pull it up to waist height. Hold the top left corner of fabric and fold it and towards the centre of your waist, tucking the fabric into your waistband. Repeat with the other side. The garment will look much like a long skirt with a pleat in the centre.

Ghana - Kente

Kente

A kente is a cloth wrap worn throughout Africa, particularly in Ghana where it is the national dress.

Material: 1 m (1 yd) of colourful fabric

Method: Hold a corner of fabric to one shoulder. Wrap fabric around the body, under the arms and bring up to meet at the shoulder again. Knot ends.

Europe - Vest

A garment that is worn by children and adults throughout the world for warmth or adornment.

Materials:
- paper grocery bags
- scissors

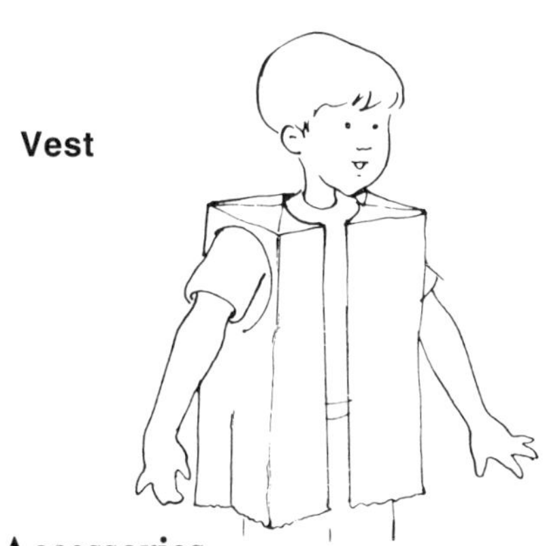

- felt-tipped pens
- crayons, paint
- craft paper, glue, gummed stickers

Method: Make vests for children by cutting out arm holes on either side of a large paper bag. Cut out an opening for the head in the centre and a slit down the front. Decorate with paint, crayons, pens, gummed stickers or with bits of cut out craft papers in a variety of colours and textures.

Accessories

Scarves - Fill your dramatic centre with a variety of scarves that can be used for veils, bandannas, head protection and pocket puffs. Include simple pieces of solid colour sheer materials, store bought designs and those you create as a class during tie dying, batikking, sponge painting or potato printing activities. Use your handcrafted scarves in these ways:

Turban

Make a turban: Wrap a long scarf around the head and pass the ends of the scarf over and under each other going around several times. When finished, tuck the ends in. **Hint:** For special events, turbans are sometimes fastened with a jewelled pin.

Headbands: Fold a rectangular scarf and tie around the head, or provide children with long pieces of plain cotton that they may paint using toothpicks and later wear as headbands. **Hint:** In some countries, such as China, headbands have been worn to display a political message; perhaps your students have an issue they would like address using their headbands.

Bandanna: Tie loosely around neck or hat.

Kerchief: Fold a square scarf in half diagonally to form a triangle. Wrap scarf over the head and tie under the chin, tucking in ends.

Some other hats to include in the dress-up centre are baseball caps, top hats, berets, rain hats, hard hats, toques, panama hats and sombreros.

Jewellery

Children all over the world wear jewellery for both decorative and symbolic reasons. Try this simple recipe for creative clay and use it to fashion your own classroom "jewels."

Materials:	- 1 cup cornstarch	250 ml
	- 2 cups baking soda	500 ml
	- 1 1/2 cups water	375 ml

Method: Stir cornstarch and baking soda together in saucepan. Add water and mix until smooth. Stir constantly and cook over medium heat until the mixture looks like mashed potatoes. Turn onto a plate and cover with a damp cloth until cool. Knead thoroughly until smooth and pliable. Mould into desired shape and dry at room temperature for 24-36 hours, turning occasionally. Apply paint when dry.

Beads

Beads are great for sorting and counting as well as for necklaces and earrings. Use the creative clay recipe and form dough into small balls and poke a hole with the sharp end of a golf tee. Let dry and apply paint. After the paint has dried string beads onto a piece of yarn or strips of leather to make necklaces and bracelets. **Hint:** You may wish to apply a protective coating of varnish.

Pendants: Mould clay into desired shape and poke a hole in the top. When dry, decorate with paint or markers and glue on decorations. Hang from a string around the neck. **Hint:** You may want to research cultural symbols and include them in your pendant design.

Other Accessory Suggestions:

Tassels: Children can make tassels and hang them from belts, masks, blankets, vests, ponchos, hats and other clothes.

Yarn Tassels

Materials: - cardboard - scissors
- yarn

Method: Cut a strip of cardboard approximately 3" x 6" (7.5 cm x 15 cm) or smaller depending on the size of tassel desired. Wrap the yarn around the cardboard. **Hint:** The more yarn used the thicker the tassel. Slip the yarn off of the cardboard and tie a short piece of yarn around the strands about 1" (2.6 cm) from the top. Cut open the bottom fold. Fluff.

Bead Tassels:

Materials: - string, yarn or strips of leather - beads
- tape

Method: Cut string, yarn or leather into 5" (13 cm) strips. Knot one end to prevent beads from slipping off and string several beads. **Hint:** To make stringing easier, wrap a piece of tape tightly around the threading end of the string. When finished, remove the tape and tie one end to the other. The bead tassles may be sewn on to various items of clothing or hung from masks as earrings or other forms of decoration.

Fans

Materials: - rectangular piece of craft paper
- felt-tipped pens or crayons
- stapler

Method: Decorate the paper with crayons or markers. Make it colourful! Create an abstract picture or a specific scene. Fold paper accordion style and staple at bottom. Fan out. **Variation:** Mix tempera paint with dish washing detergent. Let children blow bubbles onto their paper with dip sticks. When the bubbles break the paint forms interesting shapes. Use a variety of paint colours and encourage children to make different sized bubbles. **Hint:** This can be a messy, but fun, activity. Be sure to cover the area in newspapers and use art aprons to protect clothing.

Leis - Found particularly in Hawaii and Polynesia, the lei necklace is a symbol of friendship and hospitality.

Materials: - tape - 30" (80 cm) string
- blunt tapestry needle - small squares of coloured tissue paper

Method: Fasten one end of the string to a table or desk with the tape and thread the needle with the string. Crumple the squares of tissue into balls. Thread the balls on the string. Fill the string with tissue "flowers." Finish by removing the needle and tape from the string and tying the ends together to form a necklace. **Hint:** Make crowns and bracelets by using shorter string.

Follow-up Activity: Research other symbols of hospitality and phrases for greetings such as "bonjour" and "aloha."

Earrings

Materials: - cardboard - felt-tipped pens
- scissors - embossed metallic paper or foil
- small beads - glue
- needle and thread or earring clips

Method: Cut out the cardboard in desired shape of earrings - circles, triangles, diamond, etc. Glue on embossed metallic paper or foil. Decorate further by gluing on beads. Glue an earring clip to the back, or using needle and thread (adult) pierce a hole in the top of the earring and make a loop large enough to fit over the ear. **Hint:** Attach several different shapes together with a piece of tape behind the earring and make long, dangling earrings.

Chapter Six
Potpourri of Ideas

- Post pictures of important people from history - both past and present. Make sure that the pictures you choose reflect a variety of racial/ethnic groups as well as a diversity of abilities.

- Decorate your classroom walls with pictures that demonstrate diversity in family make-up - single mothers and fathers, extended families, gay or lesbian families, interracial families, differently abled family members, nuclear families, etc.

- Make a chart titled "Jobs at My House" and have the children list the jobs that they may have at home. Ask questions such as "Who does the dishes at your house?", "Who does the laundry?". Examine different ways people undertake similar tasks.

- Design your own multicultural puzzles! Choose pictures that accurately represent different ethnic groups. Glue onto a sheet of cardboard and cut into different shapes to form a puzzle. **Hint:** Title each puzzle and store in labeled envelopes.

- Create language puzzles. Write an everyday word onto a large index card or piece of cardboard. On the opposite side of the card write the word in a different language. For example, use the words "water/agua" or "hello/bonjour". Cut the card into pieces forming a puzzle.

- Place pictures of various dwellings and other buildings in the block area and encourage students to build a variety of structures, for example, an Iroquois Longhouse or Jewish Sukkah.

- Include books in your library that have been written in more than one language.

- Learn the names of colours, numbers, or days of the week in different languages. **Hint:** Parents can be a great source of information. Write down the words and display in your room. Use these words with the children on a daily basis.

- Research manners cross-culturally to help remove ignorance about why some people may respond in certain ways. For example, in some countries it may be a compliment to be whistled at by a crowd during a sports event, in others it may be seen as insulting.

- Research poetry and nursery rhymes from other cultures. Try writing your own as a class project.

- Invite a grandparent, parent or community member into your classroom to share a recipe, story or particular skill.

- Body labelling activity: Have children work co-operatively in pairs tracing each others body onto a sheet of newsprint. Label body parts in two or more different languages using index cards on which you have pre-written the words as points of reference.

- Read myths and legends from many cultures. Have the children write their own or work together to develop a story. Dramatize your tale, creating costumes and props.

- Birthdays are celebrated in many different ways. In some cultures the first birthday is considered the most important, in other groups a party is given when an infant is one week old, and some people throw the biggest celebrations for every tenth birthday! Research these and many other birth or name day celebrations with your students. Make a chart of the activities your students enjoy at parties. Throw a birthday party for the class!

- Celebrate the birthday of someone famous - Martin Luther King, Ghandi, or Dr. Seuss, to name a few. Use these celebrations as a springboard into other subjects such as civil rights, world peace or favourite authors by researching the person whose birthday you will be celebrating.

- Tell multicultural stories during circle time. Look up fairy tales from around the world in your local library (Dewey Decimal No. 398.2).

- Make your environmental print multilingual. The reference centre in your library has dictionaries in many languages. Look up words like window, door, piano, light, shelf, etc. in as many languages as possible and post these labels around the classroom.

- Plan a unit about fantasy creatures from around the world - Irish Leprechauns, Chinese Dragons, English Fairies, Russian Giants, Norwegian Mermaids, North American Sasquatch, African Anansi.

- Many fairy tales from around the world share common characters or themes. Read two or more versions of a similar story (such as Cinderella) and make a chart of similarities and differences.

- When using visual aids during storytelling, ensure that the aids you have chosen are accurate depictions of real people. For example, use flannelboard figures of people with different body shapes, sizes and abilities.

- Use people coloured paper to create puppets. This is particularly important when making community helper figures that accurately reflect different races and cultures present in the workforce.

- Provide hair coloured yarn for craft projects involving people.

- Use black and brown playdough along with the other colours.

- Include skin coloured crayons in with the other coloured crayons.

- Avoid using black paint to represent angry or negative feelings or emotions.

- Fill your art centre with a variety of coloured paper for craft projects as opposed to only using white paper.

- Provide a variety of musical instruments on a regular basis, for example, rhythm sticks, guitars, flutes, drums, gongs, rattles, maracas, and tlukeres.

- Include props to make your folk tales come alive at story time. **Some suggestions:** Origami figures, felt figures for the flannelboard, different coloured sock puppets or wooden puppets.

- Have a wide variety of dolls available in your dramatic centre. Include a relevant number and variety of dolls of colour. Use dolls in a variety of forms of dress and have girl dolls that wear pants as well as dresses. Also, include differently abled dolls.

- Provide props in your dramatic centre that portray white and blue collar occupations. Include briefcases, hard hats, lunch boxes, aprons, tools, etc.

- Demonstrate different methods of completing daily chores in your dramatic centre. Provide a washboard, bar of soap, or wash tub containing a large stone and water to use when cleaning clothes. Add a clothesline and clothes pegs.

- Research different ways of playing common games like hopscotch, hide-and-seek, and jump-rope. Create your own version of these games within your classroom culture.

- Play music and songs of different ethnic groups and in different languages.

- Learn simple songs and finger-plays in different languages or from a variety of cultures.

- Make wall collages of pictures that show children from many different racial and ethnic groups doing similar activities such as eating, playing and helping others.

- Research toys from around the world. How are they different? How are they the same? For example, look at different types of spinning tops and kinds of dolls.

- Using skin toned crayons, help children make self-portraits. Hang from a bulletin board titled "We All Have Beautiful Colours."

-Begin a pen pal program. Perhaps some children in your class have a relative or know of someone in a different community who would like to exchange correspondance. Send photographs, letters and newspaper clippings to each other.

- Keep a camera handy to record different activities and classroom events. Post the pictures on a special bulletin board. This is particularly important in promoting a sense of group identity in your classroom.

- Make photocopies of your class picture and make these available to students for use in art and writing centres. They may cut out pictures of classmates to use in their illustrations and stories.

- Display pictures that depict the elderly of various backgrounds participating in different activities.

- Include in your picture-files some photographs and illustrations of differently abled people of various backgrounds doing work or recreation.

- In your language arts centre provide examples of different languages to hear or see, including sign language and Braille.

- Learn forms of greeting in a variety of languages and use these as your students arrive each day.

- Look at royalty around the world and the different names used for the ceremonial and practical heads of government.

- Listen to different national anthems from countries around the world.

- After studying the flags of the world, students can design and make their own flags.

- Pets are very important to children. Look at different kinds of pets from around the globe.

- Sign out multicultural cookbooks from the library for use in your classroom kitchen centre.

- Buy small amounts of foreign currencies from the bank, laminate and post on walls.

- Write to foreign embassies for information and photographs of their country - but be aware of bias.

- Connect with another school in a different part of the country or world. Trade photographs, recipes, stories, etc.

- Make colour photocopies or buy prints of famous art-work from around the world and post them on your walls.

- Not all countries use cars as the major form of transportation. Study transportation methods in England, Japan, Australia, Denmark, Saudia Arabia, etc.

- Look at different ways children may get to school within your community and throughout the world. For example, some children may arrive by boat, trolley, bus, snowmobile, ferry, bicycle, pony, car, etc.

- Make your students aware of their community by bringing in a copy of the local newspaper. Highlight articles about different cultures and children.

- Make a community newspaper book. Cut out relevant articles and mount on construction paper. Bind the sheets together and put the book in your reading centre.

- Buy and display newspapers from other communities and countries. Read appropriate articles during circle time.

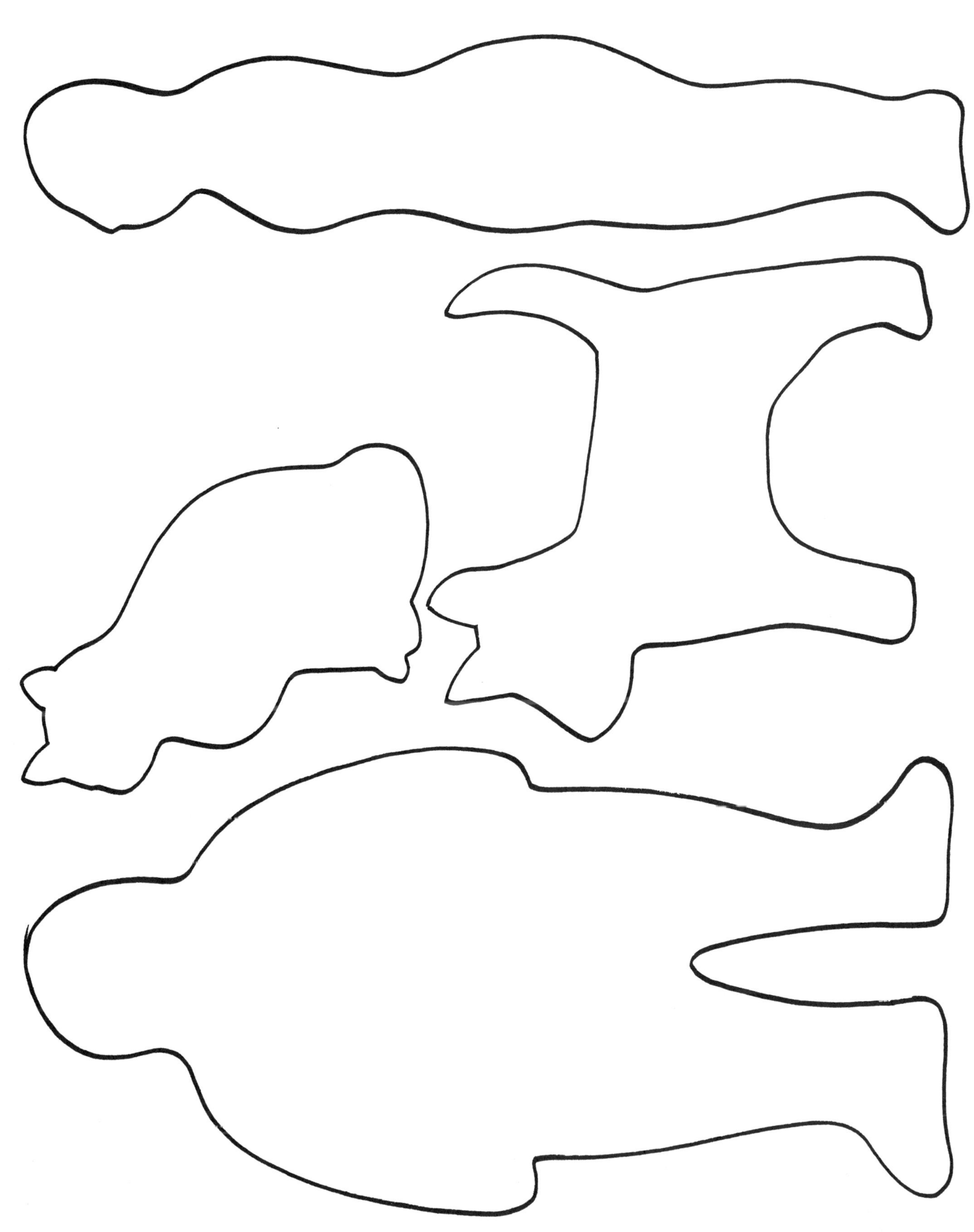